Minim

Organize Your Home and Y
Following Practical Strategies for Decluttering and Organizing

By Matt McKinney

© **Copyright 2019 - All rights reserved.**

The content contained within this book may not be reproduced, duplicated or transmitted without direct written permission from the author or the publisher.

Under no circumstances will any blame or legal responsibility be held against the publisher or author for any damages, reparation, or monetary loss due to the information contained within this book. Either directly or indirectly.

Legal Notice:

This book is copyright protected. This book is only for personal use. You cannot amend, distribute, sell, use, quote or paraphrase any part, or the content within this book, without the consent of the author or publisher.

Disclaimer Notice:

Please note the information contained within this document is for educational and entertainment purposes only. All effort has been executed to present accurate, up to date and reliable, complete information. No warranties of any kind are declared or implied. Readers acknowledge that the author is not engaging in the rendering of legal, financial, medical or professional advice. The content within this book has been derived from various sources. Please consult a licensed professional before attempting any techniques outlined in this book.

By reading this document, the reader agrees that under no

circumstances is the author responsible for any losses, direct or indirect, which are incurred as a result of the use of information contained within this document, including, but not limited to, —errors, omissions, or inaccuracies.

Table of Contents

Introduction 1

Chapter 1: Your Stuff Doesn't Have to be a Burden 4

    Applying Minimalistic Principles to the Design of Your Home 5

    Fighting Materialism with Minimalism 7

Chapter 2: How to Start with a Minimalist Lifestyle 10

    Declutter! 10

    Get Rid of the Boxes 11

    Manage Your Cables 13

    One In, One Out Rule 13

    Getting Rid of Things 14

Chapter 3: Minimalist Lifestyle is About Freedom 16

    Create s Space for Zen 17

    Reduce Your Cleaning Time 18

    Achieve Financial Freedom 19

Chapter 4: By Choosing to Be a Minimalist, You Will Be More Productive 22

    Design Your Home Office 23

    Make Sure That Your Electronics Remain Clean and Fast 26

Chapter 5: Create Room for Things Which are Important and Which Deserve It 28

    Turn Your Home Into Your Ally 29

    How to Resist the Temptation to Buy Unnecessary Clutter 30

    Have a List 31

Chapter 6: You are Helping the Environment by Being a Minimalist 32

- Achieve Self-sufficiency 32
- How to Simplify Your Lifestyle in Order to Benefit the Environment . 34

Chapter 7: By Saving More Money, You Will be Rewarded by Being Able to Buy Nicer Things 35
- Create an Amazing Home With Less 35
- Always Stay Authentic and Keep Your Creativity Alive 37

Chapter 8: A Large Home Isn't Necessarily a Key to Happiness 39
- Minimalistic Living and Budgeting 40

Chapter 9: Stop the Comparison Game 43
- Learn to be Patient 45

Chapter 10: Being a Minimalist Will Make You Happier 47
- How Can You Achieve Happiness Through Minimalism 47
- More Freedom 49
- The Power of Gratitude 49

Conclusion 52

Thank you for purchasing this book and I hope that you will find the principles of minimalism useful so that you could get what you want and be happy and fulfilled. If you will like this book and you want to share your thoughts, then you can do so by leaving a review on the Amazon page. It helps me out a lot.

Introduction

It is way too easy for anyone that is living in today's world to think about never having enough and always needing more in order to achieve happiness. It is easy to spend way too much time and energy imagining having more possessions and stuff in order to alleviate a sense of emptiness inside and absorbing magazines and TV shows and thinking that having more is always the answer.

This envy is only made stronger by various programs on MTV, by countless magazines about interior design and by countless Youtube videos which showcase room after room which all seem to be designed with the sole purpose of stimulating envy and making us eternally unhappy with what we currently have.

When life inevitably gets hard and when we get overwhelmed, it is hard to not think about how better it would all be and how happier we would all be if we had more. Having more always seems like a solution for everything.

To a lot of people, this may sound like truth, but what is ironic is that all of this is false and that the solution for most people would be needing and wanting fewer things and that would actually make them happier. Minimizing a lifestyle is what will enable people to create more space and to actually own more attractive possessions and to enjoy and appreciate the items that are currently in possession of a whole lot more.

You may find this tough to believe, but you already, at this moment, have everything you need in order to create this kind of life and you don't need any extra expense in order to do so. Your family and friends will actually be the ones that are envious when you are done applying what is taught within this book. The home that you own right now can be turned into what you are seeing in media and in order to achieve this, you don't need to buy anything. On the contrary, what you have to do is to get rid of certain things.

After doing this for some time, you will realize that you have actually discovered the way forward by getting rid of the clutter from your life and giving more appreciation toward the things you already own. Doing this will make you into a lot happier person too.

By reading through this book, you can learn how to make these things happen for you and how to make your home so awesome that people visiting your home may think that it is a home of an interior design guru. Doing this may sound expensive, but you will actually be saving a lot of money by doing so. The home that you create this way will support your desired lifestyle and your life will be so much smoother and you will enjoy it a lot more. Along with all the other benefits, your mindset and your perspective will go through a positive transformation that will make happiness so much easier by having a deep appreciation for things that you already have.

By reading through this book, you will learn about how to create your space of zen which will provide you with relaxation that everyone needs. You will also learn how to be more efficient and to make the most out of the things in your vicinity and this is how you will turn your home into a luxurious living space. You will also learn to recognize what is important since that is the only way of decluttering your life and organizing your home and your life. By living like this, you will be saving a lot of money and you will be protecting your environment since you aren't needlessly wasting things.

Your mindset will also take a drastic shift and envy will be a foreign concept for you since you will know how to really appreciate the things which you already own. You will also learn how to create efficient systems which will allow you to reduce the time that would be spent on menial valueless tasks so that you can spend time on what you value the most. By doing this, your level of stress will plummet. You will ultimately learn the true purpose of minimalism and how to incorporate minimalistic principles into your life to transform it for the better.

Chapter 1: Your Stuff Doesn't Have to be a Burden

What does living a minimalist lifestyle mean? Is it more than just another variant of interior design? What is the meaning behind it all? It is about getting everything you ever wanted by realizing you had it all along. Minimalistic life boils down to decluttering and getting rid of non-essentials. It is about reducing your possessions and about the efficiency of doing more with less. Minimalism is a deep appreciation of a couple of things as opposed to a shallow orientation towards many things which you may not even want or care about.

A lot of successful companies such as Apple actually apply minimalistic principles to the design of their products and their devices. Everything has to have a purpose and a reason for being a part of the design and that is why Apple's products aren't overdecorated or overdesigned.

For example, a website design doesn't require complex background or a myriad of menus and it doesn't have to be filled up to the brim with stuff. Everything that is placed on a website should be done so with a purpose and a clear goal and it is necessary to know what wants to be accomplished in order to do this successfully. If the goal is getting the attention of website visitors to a certain element of a website, then the design should accommodate that. It should be clear what is important and what is attempted to be communicated. The button on a website has to have a purpose and the last thing that you want to do is to design a website equivalent of a TV remote.

Applying Minimalistic Principles to the Design of Your Home

These same principles can be applied to the design of your own home although it may not be necessary to communicate something through design or to try to send a profound message.

The furniture which is designed according to minimalistic principles is quite distinct, and when you are looking at such furniture, you can clearly see that there is no unnecessary decoration or a design which doesn't have a reason for being there. Every element of such furniture has a clear purpose and it is all about practicality.

Now that you know how minimalists think about their furniture, now you know what to look for when trying to create a minimalistic home. Now you will be more likely to get rid of the unnecessary stuff and you also won't be tempted to add in more stuff just for the sake of adding stuff. You will also be better at immediately recognizing what is important when a choice is made about furniture.

The reasons why minimalistic design principles have gotten more and more popular are the practicality and improvements of interactions. The minimalistic approach is a more effective design approach since there are fewer distractions and the visitors of a website know precisely what to do and where to go since they are directed to a place where the desired interactions are encouraged. The minimalistic design philosophy when it comes to a website isn't concerned with cramming as many elements as possible since minimalists know that space actually creates calmness and peace. These same principles can be actually applied to the design of your home and by removing what is unnecessary and decluttering, it makes living in your home a lot simpler. By having fewer things and fewer elements, it will be easy and quick to find what you are looking for and hours of life can be saved by doing this over the course of time.

The less clutter there is in a certain place, the less things there are to keep track of and this will provide the eyes with a much-needed rest and restoration. This is what ensures that your home has a sense of peace and calmness and the relaxation and all the other activities will be performed so much smoother.

All this means that you are investing less of your valuable time in mundane tasks such as tidying up and looking for a thing you are trying to find. Your home will be clean and nice to look at most of the time and you will have more time and energy than ever before to dedicate to things that matter to you and that bring you joy.

Similar to UI, your home has a specific role and that role is making sure that your lifestyle is being supported. You need to know if there is a reason for a certain item to be within your home and if there is no good reason you can think of, then that item needs to go. You will breathe so much more easily when your home is designed in this way.

Fighting Materialism with Minimalism

More people than ever are beginning to realize that having fewer things and having fewer possessions can be beneficial. Because of this, people tend to be happier with what they already have and they are less prone to marketing messages which are telling them that they have to buy every single thing that is advertised in order to be fulfilled.

People who focus on less tend to be happier and more satisfied and this is very important since now it is possible to be intrinsically happy since less thought will be given towards thinking about all of the stuff that is lacking.

By adopting this sort of lifestyle, you will also keep your costs down and you will actually have more money to spend on things and experiences that you actually value and which bring you joy. By doing this, you are taking a stance against modern consumeristic culture. This approach is actually quite similar to what many philosophies preached about for a long time. The fact is that happiness comes from gratitude and from appreciating what you do have instead of focusing on what you don't have.

You have probably heard about rich people who seemingly have it all, but are still under stress and are not happy. The reason for that is the fact that they are stretching their budget to the limit in order to support their lifestyle. It can be very easy to get used to a certain way of living and this is especially true if it took a lot of money and a lot of hard work to make that happen. It takes a humongous amount of work in order to make and to maintain such a lifestyle and it can be way too easy to get caught up in the loop of thinking about what a person doesn't have and what is missing.

It is necessary to sometimes stop and to smell the roses and to actually enjoy and appreciate what is there since there is a lot of value and beauty there and it is shame to not notice it and to get lost in the noise. Minimalism can teach you how to get the most out of what you are currently working with and this applies to all areas of life. It is necessary to have a grateful attitude since only then it is possible to appreciate the people and the things around you. Gratitude is what takes happiness to a whole new level when a person realizes the value of the important things such as health and people around them. People that do this are a lot less likely to try to keep up with the Joneses and to always be envious of the grass that is apparently greener on the other side.

Being present is a lot more important instead of mindlessly spending money on things that bring minimal value. Minimalists don't link happiness with what they own and they see their possessions for what they really are. Minimalists enjoy just being able to be with their mind and being able to experience life and they don't let the minor things ruin their whole day.

There are a lot of good things that can be enjoyed in life and they can be enjoyed right now if a choice to do so is made. It is necessary to know how to stop and to appreciate what is here right now instead of always thinking about the next thing or the next fancy toy. People who never have enough are more likely to work more hours and to take loans and those are ultimately short term strategies and what those people have to realize consciously is that they already have everything they need to be happy and that they just need to stop and to reach out and grab it.

By studying the works of great philosophers, it is easy to spot those same conclusions as a recipe for happiness. It is necessary to stop and to appreciate what a person has and by doing this, a lot of stress, dissatisfaction and distractions won't be an issue anymore. This is all easier said than done in a developed world where it seems that every company under the sun is trying to show how awesome their products are and why people can't do without them. However, it is easier with the right knowledge and that is what this book is all about.

Chapter 2: How to Start with a Minimalist Lifestyle

A lot of people throughout the world are living the lifestyle that isn't even close to what is described in this book. There is a good chance that every inch of free space is covered by some clutter and people that live in such homes probably have an extensive list of additional things they want and that they won't think twice about spending their hard earned cash on. There is nothing wrong with wanting the quality of life, but it has to be deserved.

If you have read up to this point, then you are aware of why always needing more and hoarding is an issue and how it won't necessarily make a person happy. It is better to start as early as possible in order to implement the necessary changes to life. Below are the steps to getting rid of the clutter and starting with the journey of a minimalist.

Declutter!

The word clutter was already used enough times in this book, but it is necessary to do so in order to stress how much of an issue it is. It is ok to have nice things, but it is important to know what is actually necessary and what isn't.

You can perform a simple experiment, go into any room in your home right now and go over any surface with your hand. It can be any surface and it doesn't really matter if it's a desk or a chair. Take a look at the items that are currently located on that surface and choose to remove half of them. This may feel unnatural and uncomfortable at first and you will probably manufacture a reason for why you need each one of those things even though you probably haven't used them in years. Still, it is necessary to remove half of them in order to continue with an experiment.

When you are done removing the items which you choose to remove, you will actually realize that the surface looks considerably better, and not just a little better. You are giving space to the items that you actually care about and this way they can stand out more since they do deserve to be able to do so. There is a good chance that you actually couldn't see the surface itself before and that you can see it now since you have eliminated a lot of clutter and this is a lot easier on the eyes and on the mind and it will make you a lot more relaxed.

The items which you decided to keep are the items that are important to you and these items are the better half. By doing this, the average value of the items and possessions that are located on that surface will go up. Now that items may get to chance to be used even more since they will look like they matter instead of just blending into the mess.

What is also neat is the fact that the cleaning will be a lot more bearable since when you have to wipe away the dust from the surface, you will only have to remove a couple of items and you will also have to only put back a couple of items when you are done. The time that will be required for cleaning will be more than cut in half and now you have more time for things that actually matter. Imagine what can be done when you apply this rule to your entire home. To take this experiment to the next level, do the same thing for every surface in a certain room of your choice.

Get Rid of the Boxes

There is a reason why removing clutter is impactful and that is because this is how you can actually get some mental space. Our brains are hard-wired to scan for something to pay attention to and to filter out the things that are worth paying attention to from the things that aren't worth the attention. If it is not easy to realize what is important and what isn't, then the brain will signal the release for more stress hormones. The more clutter and noise there is, the harder the brain has to work to process all that information and this can lead to burnout, especially if a person is tired after a tough day when all a person wants to do is to relax.

More clutter means more work and this is why more isn't always better when it comes to the amount of stuff in our lives and our homes. There are a lot of seemingly innocent items which are causing you stress even if you may not realize that and one example of such items are various boxes that you probably have all around your home. You are probably convinced that boxes are a great item to have since they will make storage that much easier and because they will enable you to get more things out of your way. The reality of the situation is that boxes also can create additional clutter and work.

Boxes will accumulate a lot of dust if they don't have a lid on. What is more important is the fact that boxes are items and items that are not necessary tend to take up space and they occupy your mind. You can perform an experiment by locating all the boxes and taking them somewhere away from your mind's eye. After you have done so, take a moment to notice how clean and how relaxing your home has become. You should search your rooms well for boxes since there is a good chance that they are located in places where it is easy to forget about them, such as under the beds or on top of the shelves.

This is simple, but the results are a lot more than simple. Only one benefit of getting rid of the boxes is the fact that future cleaning will be so much easier and so much faster. You should take time to figure out what in your home causes stress and an increase in the noise, even though you may not consider it as clutter.

Manage Your Cables

Cables are one thing that even people that aren't minimalists get really annoyed with and it is important to manage those cables in some way in order to avoid cable horror. There is a good chance that you have cables in your home which you have completely given up on as far as organization is concerned.

However, these cables do have a potential for creating clutter for the eyes and your home can seem a lot less tidy and organized if they aren't handled properly. Thankfully, there are ways to manage those pesky cables and boxes can be actually used for storing those cables. You can also attach those cables to the underside of the desk and to attach them to the back of the equipment such as monitors. A proper solution for cables will be different for everyone and, therefore, it is necessary to get creative in order to create more space.

One In, One Out Rule

If you want to ensure that your home remains uncluttered, you need to establish certain rules and you need to stick to them. „One in, one out" rule is one rule which you should definitely be sticking to in order to achieve the goal of keeping an uncluttered home. This rule is simple and it consists of getting rid of one item for each new item that you buy and this will make sure that you keep the number of your possessions under control so that you wouldn't fall victim to burnout.

By doing this, you will also be saving money if you make an effort to sell the item that you are getting rid of. In this way you don't have to concern yourself with creating additional space for a new item since every time you buy a new item, a necessary space is created. Practicing this rule will force you to really think about which things are important to you and worth keeping.

This rule could sound a bit extreme, but you should just try it out and once you see the results, then there won't be a doubt in your mind about this rule being the right thing to follow.

Getting Rid of Things

Just by implementing these tips, you will realize that you are getting rid of a surprising number of things. It is necessary to mention again that this process isn't easy. Change is not easy for most people.

In order to start, you should start with a bang and you should do a large declutter where you quickly get rid of a lot of stuff. This is a good way to reset your home and your life and it gives you a fresh start. This is really powerful since people love the sense of a new beginning and a new adventure.

The first step to decluttering is filling up the boxes with things that have been sitting in the storage for too long and that will likely not be used again. If something hasn't been used in 6 months or more, then it should go in the box. The things that hold sentimental value or which are very monetarily valuable are an exception to this rule, however.

The crucial tip to getting rid of things is to do it quickly since you may hesitate and quick altogether if you stop and think for too long. Before you start discarding, you should see if any of the items could be sold for a decent price, and if they can, then you want to keep those so that you can sell them as soon as possible. Everything that is left can either be donated to a charity or thrown out for good.

As far as selling items is concerned, don't try to sell each item since going through each item and evaluating it will create additional stress and this only increases the chances of abandoning the whole process.

Chapter 3: Minimalist Lifestyle is About Freedom

If you are still not sure if minimalism is a good choice, then just think of how hard it will be to move with a lot of possessions. Moving and changing homes with a lot of clutter and a lot of stuff isn't fun and this is the situation where all the stuff that you don't need will come to bite you in the butt.

The goal is to reduce the things which you own to the essentials which you can't do without and to things that you love and which are meaningful to you. When you do that, moving will be exponentially easier and faster. Moving is not easy and it is not necessary to make it even tougher.

Doing this also gives you an option of putting all your belongings in a backpack and traveling the world at your own leisure. The world is your oyster when you can do this. You can also rent out your home as you travel in order to truly be efficient.

This is one example of how having less clutter actually provides you with freedom. Traveling the world in this way simply wouldn't be nearly as possible if you had a lot of stuff weighing you down. You simply can't be as flexible when you have a lot of stuff and it is, pretty much, akin to being anchored. I can promise you that you will feel light as a feather when you have less mess in your life weighing you down.

Create s Space for Zen

There are a lot of ways in which having less stuff can be liberating and one more example of that is the fact that less stuff means less stress. It can be said that a home is a reflection of the owner's mindset. Life will get busy for anyone at certain times and the home can be a reflection of a situation when it feels like the weight of the world is on top of the owner. It can be easy for clutter to accumulate all around and it can seem impossible to get around to actually managing that clutter.

The sink may be full of dishes or the papers could be lying around and it can be very hard to relax in such circumstances, and even when a time for relaxing does come, it is hard to actually get the most out of that relaxation since the messiness of the home acts as a reminder of all the issues.

When the home is messy, there is always a lingering feeling about chores having to be done. This makes it additionally harder to relax properly and to put your mind at ease.

Even if you are doing everything very well as far as being a minimalist is concerned, there will still be situations in which not everything is as it should be and these situations will inevitably cause you to get stressed since things are not happening according to your expectations. In order to combat this, you should create your space of Zen and this will be any place or a room within your home where there will never be any mess. Design in that room will be even more minimalistic and that will be accomplished with the addition of even more rules such as no food or drinks being allowed inside or not being allowed to enter wearing shoes.

The goal of having such a place within your house that will always be neat and organized no matter what happens is to make sure that you always have a place where you will be able to just sit down and to shut off the rest of the world while you do some unwinding activity such as reading a book.

Reduce Your Cleaning Time

As mentioned earlier, you will be spending a lot less time cleaning up when you live like a minimalist and this will additionally minimize the amount of mundane work that is necessary to keep things as they should be since you are using efficient systems.

It is a fact that most people spend more time than they would like performing tasks that aren't really engaging but have to be done such as doing the laundry or dishwashing or ironing the clothes or any other chore. These activities can take away the time which you could be spending on fulfilling activities such as spending time with people that matter to you, or doing something important such as writing a book.

A lot of tedious parts of life will be reduced by becoming a minimalist and doing something as simple as having fewer possessions will drastically reduce the time which you would otherwise have spent cleaning up. The same principles could be applied to any other possession you may have and this will also contribute to reducing the time spent doing chores so that same time could be put into something you value.

If you want to take all of this a step further, you should have systems in place which will ensure that the work goes a lot more smoothly. For example, investing upfront into a dishwasher could eliminate the chore of having to manually clean the dishes and while the whole chore of dish cleaning is being done by the machine, you can do something else like dealing with some other chore. Dishwashers cost money upfront, but they will save you time, and you have to realize a lot of choices in life boil down to a tradeoff between time and money.

You can create systems for a lot of other things such as paperwork so that you could organize them in as little time as possible. You can also make a plan for the clothes that you will wear so that you have to make fewer decisions which will make sure that you avoid decision fatigue. There is a reason why a lot of successful people use this life hack.

You have, without a doubt, seen one of those robotic vacuum cleaners and investing in one of those is also smart if you really want to cut down on the time spent vacuuming.

To summarise the point of all these examples, minimalism isn't just about how things look, it is also about making sure that a certain place requires minimal upkeeping and maintenance which no one really likes to do and this can even include choosing foods which take less time to prepare even though they may not taste as good as some other options which would require longer preparation time.

Achieve Financial Freedom

Maybe the most important thing about being a minimalist is the fact that you can buy yourself a good chunk of financial freedom since you have fewer requirements and fewer things which you just have to have. This means that your expenses are significantly lower and the amount of money you need in order to achieve happiness is a lot lower. This will make your life a lot easier and a lot more enjoyable since you won't be so financially worried since you won't have as much debt which would have to force you to do the things which you don't want to do.

The wealth isn't only about how much money you bring in; it is about the difference between the money you bring in and the money you spend. Obviously, by reducing the amount of money that you spend, your wealth will go way up and that is what will give you options in life.

After reading through this chapter, it should be clear to you how you don't need to accumulate stuff in your life in order to be fulfilled and to make your home a pleasant place to live in. Even though that not buying countless unnecessary things is a piece of good advice, it is still advisable to sell things which you don't have a use for anymore and this will be really helpful as far as saving cash is concerned. If you are reading this, there is a good chance that you are a smartphone user, and if you care about always having the latest model, then you can trade in your current model for the latest one when the time comes and you will be able to get the latest model with minimal cost when the time comes.

In the same way, you can also save a lot of money by using what you already have and being resourceful instead of constantly buying new things. In order to implement this, you should know ahead of time what you like doing in order to be able to do what you want. As a result, you can focus more of your time and energy on meaningful things such as reading books.

If there is some way to make your life more simple by still keeping things and activities you care about, then do so. By applying what is described in this chapter, you will save loads of money over the long term and you will be able to live without a worry knowing that you don't have to worry about debt or wondering if you can actually afford something that would make you happy. This carefree kind of living will make sure that you are so much more comfortable than what you would be by having a lot of stuff.

Your whole life can be designed by using the principles I just outlined and by adopting this kind of thinking, you will automatically consider getting a smaller house instead of a larger one if that means that your mortgage installments will be lower which will ensure that you keep more money and therefore more freedom.

Chapter 4: By Choosing to Be a Minimalist, You Will Be More Productive

Have you ever thought about how many things which you own you don't even use or don't even know the purpose of? Does this realization make you more stressed?

Now let's imagine the opposite situation: You are completely aware of all of your possessions and you can very quickly remember all the things that you own and the reason for owning those things. Doesn't this second situation feel so much better? This approach will actually provide you with a lot more energy and a lot less stress and your productivity will skyrocket as a result. This may be subtle, but the chances are high that the mess and the lack of organization in your home impact your productivity in a negative way.

If you want to be able to do good work, then you have to make sure that you intentionally design your working space. This doesn't have to be complicated since complexity is the enemy of execution. For example, when your home is more pleasant, then you will be more likely to stick to your hygienic habits and your other healthy habits that have to get done.

When you have to search every corner and every drawer to find what you want, that adds up over the course of days and weeks and you can lose a lot of your time and energy which will ensure that your life will take a hit. This chapter is all about showing you how being more minimalistic can improve your productivity with your work and all areas of life.

Design Your Home Office

When most people think about being productive at home, they will think of something like a personal office within their homes where they keep all necessary things for doing the work such as a computer or relevant files and all the other items that may be helpful. It is necessary to plan and to know what may be necessary for the work so that you don't get interrupted by having to look for things that aren't within the reach of your hand.

If you are fortunate enough to have a career which allows you to work from home, or if you just like to have space within your home where you do your administrative duties, then this chapter will prove to be quite helpful.

For the most people, this office space within a home will not be very tidy and organized and it will look like a bomb went off when you see all the papers and tools and cables lying around.

In order to get this organized, you need to make sure that you have a system for organizing your documents. The good old filing cabinet will do the trick here. You do have to know which documents are actually appropriate for filling since there are some documents which you may need to use more frequently. You can achieve this kind of organization by using paper trays and you should use those while keeping how human memory works in mind.

You should have one tray which is used for all the current projects which are handled right at the moment of working. This tray should be dealt with every day and it is necessary to get rid of things that shouldn't be there anymore by either getting rid of them or putting them on another tray.

At the end of the work week, which will most likely be Friday, you will take anything that is still left on the current tray and you will place it in the filing cabinet if you deem it important enough while throwing away anything else that is considered unimportant. This is effective because it is acknowledged that there are some things that may require quick access and recovery. Also, by sticking to this system over the course of time, you make sure that the paperwork doesn't pile up and that it is put where it won't be able to create a mess.

If you can, then you should make an effort to reduce the quantity of paper you are working with. You should always have some kind of notepad with you so that you could capture ideas before they disappear and you should always think if converting a certain document to a digital format makes sense and you should do so if you determine that digitalization is the best choice.

By doing this, the organization will be so much easier. It is also a good idea to invest in a scanner which you can use to scan important documents so that you could convert them into a file that will be possible to work with on a computer. If you think that a physical form of the scanned document is no longer necessary, then you can simply get rid of it.

If you implement these changes into your system, the work which is required for paperwork all around your home will be much easier to manage and that will ensure that your home makes it easier for you to be productive.

Again, knowing how to manage your cables is pretty important. If it is possible to use a wireless variant for certain electronics, then you should do so since it will make your life so much easier. If you are really serious about this, then you can purchase a product such as Amazon Echo which will allow you to issue voice commands to your computer.

In order to be more productive, it is all about making the procedures simpler and removing the obstacles and doing this fairly regularly. The fewer steps there are to completing a certain task, the more efficient a system is. Everything that you may require to do your work should be within your reach and this is a variant of French cooking concept known as mise en place. Designing your home like this will save you hours.

The goal of removing clutter and obstacles is to make getting the work done easier and smoother. If a certain item or a certain piece of furniture doesn't serve a purpose within your office, then you should get rid of it from your office to make things easier for you. Any extra items that are in your office have the potential to be a distraction and that is why you should carefully consider what is in your office and what isn't. You want to make a separation between your working life and your personal life and doing this actually resets your brain.

The place in which the work is done shouldn't be used to do fun things and that is why a bookshelf or a TV has no reason for being there since that will only put ideas of fun in your head. The room in which you do your work shouldn't necessarily be bland and it is actually a good idea to add some color to that room if that will help your productivity. When choosing a color, remember that certain colors are better for productivity instead of others and light green, for example, is relaxing since it is similar to what you would see when looking at plants and that simply feels good.

The point is that if you don't like corporate looking environments, then you shouldn't design your working space as one. Just make sure that the room in which you do work doesn't have things which have the potential to distract you and this will make procrastination a whole lot harder. Using each line of defense against procrastination is necessary.

Make Sure That Your Electronics Remain Clean and Fast

It is important for a piece of technology to keep doing its job well and without hiccups. Just as you want to make sure that the room in which you are doing your work is nice and tidy and without clutter, you want to apply the same logic and the same rules to the computer you are working on. If the desktop of your computer is covered with icons that you don't use, then that is also an issue for productivity since that will stress you out. That could also slow down your computer and that will also cause a lot of stress which will ruin your productivity plans.

You want to take the organization of your files seriously since you don't want for important files to go missing. You also don't want for your computer to be too slow since that will make you anxious each and every time you boot up your computer. The minimalistic design principles are not limited to only your room and you should be applying them to the design of your computer as well. If there is an unnecessary file, then you want , and you also want to make sure that your antivirus software is a good one. You also want to know if there is a good reason for installing a particular piece of software. It is extremely satisfying when your computer is running as it should and when you are not being taken out of the flow of the work by a slow computer.

Chapter 5: Create Room for Things Which are Important and Which Deserve It

In order to be successful with the implementation of minimalistic principles, it is necessary to really think about what you want to achieve in your life and what kind of home design has to be achieved to make sure that your goals are achieved.

You don't want to be in a situation where your home is an obstacle to working toward your goals and to working effectively and efficiently. It should be the opposite, your home is what should make things easier for you so that you have a better chance of accomplishing what you want.

The question you may be asking now is why does it happen that so many people don't utilize this philosophy of home and life design? The answer to that is actually quite simple and it boils down to the fact that some people simply don't know what they want from their home and from life as a whole. One thing that could be blamed for all this is media and marketing since they are constantly showing us a supposedly better way to live which is better than what we are currently doing. This makes it hard to be satisfied and to know what you actually want. As a consequence, it is easy to get lost in a sea of different marketing agendas and goals. It is really hard to be truly happy when we are constantly hearing about a better way to do something.

In order to not fall for anything, you need to stand for something. You need to sit down and to really think about what is important to you and what you want to get out of life since you can't get what you want if you don't know what you want. You should write down an affirmation based on what you want and you can start to build your ideal home by using that as a guide. The point is that you don't want to be without the knowledge of what goals are important and the strategies for moving towards those goals.

Turn Your Home Into Your Ally

Maybe you came to the realization that what you really value the most in your life are the people close to your and music. Now that you have this knowledge, you can start designing your Home appropriately. For example, you may design your home in a way that accommodates guests so that they want to spend more time there. The rooms which would go a long way towards accomplishing these design goals would be some form of entertainment rooms such as rooms with comfy furniture and a large television accompanied with a large table for all the snacks. As far as the love of music is concerned, you could design a room completely for that and select the most appropriate decorations.

In both of these examples, you are making a decision about the design based on your whether or not a certain purchase will get you closer or further from what you are trying to achieve. You are also considering if a certain decision will bring joy or not. You also begin to include more dimensions into your decision-making process such as an opportunity cost and whether a purchase of something is an objective improvement.

When you think like this, then it will be much harder for you to be influenced by marketing campaigns since you clearly know what you want and you won't be satisfied until you are successful in achieving that. That is easier said than done however and there are still certain urges to resist.

How to Resist the Temptation to Buy Unnecessary Clutter

When you are considering making a purchasing decision, you should have a checklist you want to run through in order to determine if a certain purchase will improve your lifestyle. Think about the long term implications of the purchasing decision.

It is also very helpful if you are educated about all the small subtle tricks which marketers tend to use in order for people to spend their money on something for which they didn't even know they wanted. When you are about to buy something, you want to use that as a trigger to slow down and to think through your decision. Most of the purchases are made emotionally and by slowing down, you can protect yourself from being too impulsive for your own good. The solution in this situation is to think logically and rationally about what you really need for your situation and by doing this over a course of time, you will be surprised at the improved quality of your decisions.

If you are going to buy something, then have a plan for the purchase beforehand and by doing so, you will not be making purchases on the spot. Whatever you were thinking about buying will likely be there and if you determine that that same thing is actually valuable, then you can go ahead with the purchase.

Have a List

There is a way to resist the temptation of buying new shiny stuff, and that is having a list of things that you really want to do. You may think that this is redundant and that you can easily keep track of everything, but the fact is that people are forgetful and that there are a lot of things that tend to get left unattended such as books that were never read or recipes that were never tried out or various activities that never seem to get their turn to be tried out. These activities can be anything from learning a new language to catching up with an old friend.

It can be easy to forget about all these things when some free time finally becomes a reality and then it can be easy to follow the path of least resistance and to simply slump in front of the TV.

It really may not be necessary to buy a new book when there are so many other books that are waiting to be read. Instead of working away in order to save money for a new TV, it can be good to remind yourself of the joy of simply going to a park or to a newly opened museum. Having a list where your ideas for an evening are listed is a really useful strategy. You can turn to that list every time you get the urge to buy something and by doing this, you will come to the realization that there are plenty of options already in your vicinity which don't require spending money, or at least not as much. You should look at your home as an ally on your path to your goals.

Chapter 6: You are Helping the Environment by Being a Minimalist

Being a minimalist doesn't just have to be about yourself and it doesn't just have to be about you wanting to make your home look better. Being a minimalist is actually good for our planet and there are many examples which can make this evident.

Take a moment to think about all the fancy gadgets which you have with yourself at all times. If you are living more like a minimalist, that means that you aren't spending that much time in front of a TV and this will reduce your costs since you won't have to pay as much for an electrical bill and the maintenance of your home as a whole.

Achieve Self-sufficiency

If there is one thing that minimalists strive for, then that goal is self-sufficiency. Minimalists need less to be happy, and therefore, happiness is much easier to achieve. A simpler life implies that you, by yourself can fulfill your needs and that way, you are freeing yourself from having to work longer hours in order to achieve a more costly lifestyle.

There are several ways to turn self-sufficiency into reality and one of those ways is to have your own garden where you will be growing your own fruits and veggies. This will provide you with what you need for health and you will also not have to spend so much at the supermarket. Doing this is also good for the environment since you are minimizing the greenhouse gas issue be creating your own ecosystem.

Another avenue of achieving self-sufficiency is by taking control of your own power and electricity. This is much easier by being a minimalist since that means that less power is required in order to keep the minimalist lifestyle up and running smoothly. Taking care of your own power is also good for the environment since you are actively reducing carbon emissions. The one mainstream option of making this work is by installing solar panels, but it is necessary to know that this option is pricey and that a lot of work is involved in getting solar panels up and running and it may require a lot of patience and waiting before seeing a return on investment.

In order to really start generating some power, you should get yourself a solar generator and you can even purchase a portable version of the solar generator. This is very important if you want to travel around since it will allow you to carry it with yourself. You will have to spare of a couple of thousands of dollars for this, although it is still a good investment and you might also get some solar panels as part of the package. All this will ensure that you have enough electricity to run your most essential electronic devices such as computers and fridges as long as nothing happens to the generator.

The generator does cost some money, but it still a better option than renovations which would also be costly.

Another trick you could use is to collect water from the rain and using some items which you can find around the house as long as they can provide you with usefulness. This is how you help yourself by reducing your spending. You will also be helping the environment since you will be wasting a lot fewer things.

How to Simplify Your Lifestyle in Order to Benefit the Environment

There are various methods which you can use to downgrade your lifestyle to the essentials which will ultimately benefit the environment. You can use your car less often since you will be saving money on fuel and you will be reducing carbon emissions. It will be pretty good for your health if you walk to places or use a bike.

In order to reduce costs further and to improve your health and the environment, you can cut down on the red meat. Red meat is pricey, but it can also be bad for the environment if it is wasted.

You can also go green and by doing this, you are giving priority to products that are made in a way that is efficient and good for the environment. If you want to signal what changes you want to see, then vote with your wallet and support green organizations. If you choose to do so, then you will get rid of a lot of clutter from your life since there will be a lot of items which you will no longer be using.

Chapter 7: By Saving More Money, You Will be Rewarded by Being Able to Buy Nicer Things

We have covered a lot of steps and tactics which can be used to edit a lifestyle and to make it more minimal with the freedom as the ultimate goal. If you have read up to this point, you have probably already thought of some ways you can apply some of these things to your situation.

It is necessary to point out that it isn't about scaling down so much that you are left with nothing. It is all about putting yourself in a position which will allow you to live life as you want it and on your terms. This isn't accomplished by getting more stuff, but rather by being resourceful and using what you already have. This is a lot safer way of getting to freedom.

In order to save money successfully, it is necessary to know what you actually want so that you wouldn't be spending automatically and unconsciously. It is not just about doing less, but about doing less and better instead of doing a million things shallowly.

A simple act of clearing the surface of things can be powerful. Imagine the added benefit of putting the things that make you happy on those surfaces. The difference is significant and noticeable in an instant. By doing small simple things such as these, you can create a pretty luxurious home.

Create an Amazing Home With Less

In order to get the home as you see in magazines, you really don't have to spend that much money. Before you start, you need to know exactly what kind of home you want and by doing this, you will be able to make a lot quicker decisions about the furniture you want.

There are actually only a couple of key features on which you want to focus on when designing a home if you want to leave a lasting impression on guests and visitors. You need to know how to select items that will complement your whole home and which will fit in well. You want to choose these things carefully since you are representing yourself through them.

For example, a neat design choice for your bathroom is to set up entry into a shower to look like when a person is entering a waterfall. Doing this can change the feel of the whole room in a good way and this will increase the level of comfort. You can also add a fireplace to your living room and this will make it a lot more comfortable to be in and it will make it more memorable.

The choice about this is completely yours and you don't want to be shy about your choices since this will only be successful as long as you are authentic. It is possible to have a pool in the garden or a chandelier, but you can only add those successfully if your design is minimal and if nonessential things are cut out. You have to know what kind of lifestyle you really want and then you want to design your home around that since that is the only way you can make things described in this chapter possible. You need to think long and hard about your priorities.

A lot of people that visit your home may leave full of envy, but the funny thing is that you may be spending less money than them. The key elements of your home really come in sharp focus when you actually remove the clutter and non-essentials which are just a distraction. This is accomplished by spending less instead of spending more.

This kind of success can be linked back to having a clear vision and knowing what you want so that you can work towards it and design your life and your living space around that. Once you know what you want, then you also know what you don't want and that is how you start cutting things out.

Always Stay Authentic and Keep Your Creativity Alive

There are a lot of opportunities to be unique and being unique and taking a stand for something means more than trying to fix an issue by throwing more money at it. Your guests will remember the visit to your place more if you show them something that is new to them. You can only do this successfully if you stay true to yourself and if you don't compromise before you achieve what you want.

You may be into working out and you could design your home around that by having your home gym, but if you really want to stand out, then you can extravagantly decorate your gym equipment and this will impress anyone that walks in. This won't cost much and it will be quite original and memorable. Anyone who sees gym like this may end up leaving full of envy since working out may seem quite fun there and that would make working out regularly so much easier.

If you want to succeed in life, you do need some creativity. You really want to think about what message you want to send through the design of your home and what idea would be behind it. You want to be keenly aware of why some things will always have a place in your home.

By thinking about this, you may come up with some alternatives which will really save you money. Maybe you have always wanted to have one of those wardrobes into which you simply walk in, but you don't have that wardrobe yet because you find it too draining on your budget. You want to really think why you want that wardrobe and what is the main reason because of which you want it. You may conclude that you just love fashion and that you love to display your good taste for everyone to see in a stylish manner.

It is great that you know why you want something, but you can achieve that same goal without necessarily buying this kind of wardrobe by being a little creative which may lead to the discovery of even better and fancier solutions than what you first envisioned.

If you buy a bookshelf, which is a lot cheaper, you could use it to display your shoes and other clothing items instead of books. In order to save even more money, you could also select a wall within your home and decorate it with shelves exclusively for your fashion.

By doing this, you will still be impressing your visitors and you will be doing it for a fraction of a price and that is a prime example of creativity and resourcefulness. Now that you have saved some money, now you can buy nice things for yourself and you can focus on your lifestyle and the things that matter to you.

Chapter 8: A Large Home Isn't Necessarily a Key to Happiness

Everyone needs to make a decision for themselves concerning how minimal they want to go and it is necessary to set some kind of boundary. Is it your goal to scale back to the fullest and to live in the wilds without any technology? Do you want to create an amazing lifestyle by using only a couple of items which will make your home look very luxurious even though it doesn't require much maintenance and upkeeping?

You need to anticipate your expenses before you make the decision. Every minimalist will have a different vision in mind when designing a lifestyle and for some, it may be about traveling while for others it may be about being financially abundant and having the option of sending kids to college stress-free.

For example, if you are someone who lives to travel, then it's quite obvious why buying a large house may not be the best choice for you. All that you need in order to achieve the lifestyle of travel is to get yourself a one-room apartment in an area which you can afford. By doing this, you have more money to do your favorite thing, which is traveling. When you live in a small home, then your minimalist capabilities will be really tested and you will really have to make some tough choices about what is important to you so that you could make the whole situation work in your favor.

Doing all these things and living like this is what the marketing industry doesn't want you to find out since people like that separate from their money less easily. As mentioned before, modern life is great, but it also attempts to manufacture demand for the things which people never wanted in the first place. It is intended to give people a boost of motivation so that they would work harder and earn more money for the corporations.

What you really do need in life is to take care of your health and to have a cozy place to stay at. If you spend some time searching and exploring, you may discover a property which is the ideal size for your needs and even if you take out a mortgage for such a property, you can pay it off in its entirety in a couple of years. You just need to be disciplined in a combination with principles of being a minimalist in order to get the things which you want and which you need to be happy for as little money as possible all in a couple of years.

The goal is to never have to worry about debt again and to find more ways to generate income so that you can quit the 9 to 5 rat race. It is possible if you want it and if you don't stop working until you get it.

Minimalistic Living and Budgeting

As it was mentioned enough times already, you need to clearly know what you want since that is the only way of you knowing what to do and which steps to take. When you have a plan, then you can take action in order to make that plan into a reality.

You need to have a budget if you want to reach your goals. This budget doesn't have to be complicated and all that you have to do is to include all your income and all your expenses and all of this you should put into an excel spreadsheet and you should do so regularly. Doing this over a course of time will give you a clear picture of your financial situation and you will be able to see if your finances are going up or down.

At the end of a certain period of time such as a week or a month, you will be able to see how much money is left and you can choose to either spend this money however you want it or you can save it.

In order to actually manage to remain consistent with this, you have to keep reminding yourself why you are doing what you are doing and you need to keep reminding yourself of your vision. Whatever your goal is, you want to know how much will your path towards your goal cost you and based on that, you could get an idea of how much time it should take you to reach a goal.

Now that you have an approximation of how much time you will need in order to reach your goal, you need to try to cut that time down and to shorten it. You can do so by reducing your costs on things which you don't actually need. You can also sell some items which you aren't even using. One more option is to reduce some other costs by eating out less or buying less things that aren't really necessary. You can also look at the list of fun and cheap activities which you have compiled before in order to keep your costs down. Just taking a walk could be so much better instead of spending an evening watching Netflix and your wallet will also love it.

Over the course of time of doing this, being more minimal will become second nature to you. The key tip for staying on track is reminding yourself of your reason for doing what you are doing. The end result of all of this is having more time and energy which you can give to the people that matter the most to you, such as your family and your friends.

Chapter 9: Stop the Comparison Game

It can be quite easy to make visitors of your home envious if you design it as it was described. There is a good reason for trying to impress visitors of the home and that is because that is what drives the purchasing decisions for most people even if they don' want to admit it. It is simply encoded into humans to be aware of their standing in the relation to other people and to always try to look at the side of their neighbors thinking the grass is greener on the other side.

Actually using the driving force of caring about what people think can be used to increase productivity and it can help them to achieve great things which could go a long way as far as increasing status is concerned. Being the leader of the pack was a huge driving force back in the day, but today it can actually lead to decreased happiness if that drive isn't controlled.

I know it may sound ridiculous, but this has been proven by psychological studies and the name of this theory is „social comparison theory" which basically states that comparison to others can have a huge impact on how happy we feel and how accomplished we feel.

One study focused on determining how happy people who earn different salaries are. It was discovered that the absolute amount of money earned didn't matter all that much. What does matter to people is how much are they earning in comparison to other people in their circle.

For example, you could be earning 150 000$ a month which is great money, but it would still be harder to be happy when you are aware at all times that other people in your circle are earning twice that amount. This kind of comparison can make you less satisfied even though you can do almost anything with that kind of money.

On the other hand, if your earnings were around 1000$ a month while everyone else was earning half of that, then you would actually feel a lot happier and accomplished. Social comparison is real and there is a good chance that it is behind a lot of wrongdoings and depression. It is a fact that a lot of people struggle with this.

It gets even worse. Before people were only comparing themselves with people in their local circle and with whom they associate daily. But today, with the world being more connected, it can seem like the whole world is one big city and now people will compare themselves to the celebrities too which may not even be on the same side of the globe. It is harder to be happy when you are constantly seeing how much fun everyone else is having on social media.

The solution is quite simple and it is to stop comparing your life to others and to snap out of it. Stop constantly trying to get the things which others have and start showing appreciation towards the things which you own already. This is easier said than done, but you really have to think about what you want and what is important to you in your life.

By doing this, it will be a lot harder to keep comparing yourself to others since you will realize that you value different things and that things which make other people happy won't necessarily make you happy. You may think you want something, but it may not improve your life in any way and it might just end up being a burden which will require maintenance which will make being happy harder.

It may take some time to rewire your mind, but eventually, you can realize that it is not important what your neighbor has since thinking like that will lead to better decision making and more happiness and fulfillment in life. You will know what is important to you and what is worth your money and that is how you make your life better and something worth being happy about.

Learn to be Patient

There is another mental shift which you need to make and that is to train your patience. Being able to delay gratification and to be patient can protect you from a lot of bad choices since you won't be getting in debt and spending money which you don't have on clutter just because you want it right now.

There is bound to be a lof rationalizing in favor of buying things right at that moment such as thinking that a certain item will be gone for good if it isn't bought right now. The main issue is in the buying habit since buying something before you can afford it means that you are likely to buy another item, in the same manner, the next week as well.

You need the discipline to be successful in life and you need to know what you want so that you would be aware of what you can and what you can't do. Doing this will ensure that your life is a lot less stressful and a lot less filled with debt which will make sure that your home is more likely to stay clean and free of clutter. You need discipline if you want to keep your life under control and in balance.

Chapter 10: Being a Minimalist Will Make You Happier

Through the course of this book, you have seen how being more minimal can allow you to have more savings, improve the environment, make your home a lot more dazzling to anyone who visits and ultimately helping you get out of the rat race so that you can live on your terms and do what you want.

All these causes are worth fighting for. Changing your thinking and decluttering your home is a good start for anyone who wants to be more fulfilled in life. Those all things are nice, but what it is ultimately about is being happy and loving life. That is possible when you decide to scale down and become minimal.

How Can You Achieve Happiness Through Minimalism

Minimalism can make people happier in two ways. Minimalism can cause a complete shift in perspective and in how people look at their possessions. This chapter is all about explaining how being minimalistic can lead to more happiness.

To recap, living a minimal lifestyle will enable you to have more time. Since your home is less cluttered, that also means that there is less cleaning up to do. If you have taken the time to figure out and to implement systems and processes so that your house could be kept clean in a way that minimizes the required maintenance.

When you are living in this way, it is so much easier to just unwind and to relax when you finally come home. It is hard to put in words how impactful it is having a simple home and it is something that needs to be experienced firsthand in order to comprehend it.

Living like a minimalist will reduce your stress. Since your lifestyle doesn't require as much money expenditure, you don't have to work as much. It is quite a realization when you figure out that you don't need to do overtime in order to get the things which you want. You will then look at so many people who trade hour after hour and wonder why someone traps themselves in such a way of life. You can be happy without needing to work more.

When you live like this, you are coming home a whole lot earlier and you are a lot more relaxed and fun to be around since you are not carrying the stress with you. There are some people that actually derive satisfaction and purpose from their work and they may be hesitant to live like this because of that, but it doesn't have to be that way and there are plenty of ways to get fulfillment from other things that aren't work. When you live like this, you can just ditch everything and go traveling to Asia for three months without having to ask anyone.

You also have an opportunity to try out something entrepreneurial and to try to figure out how to make money online. Since you have fewer things that you have to attend to around the house and because of that, you will be less pressured to go after money at the expense of other areas of life. You can only be out of balance for so long.

If something does go wrong, which it inevitably does, you aren't short on savings which you can use to make a problem, such as a boiler issue, go away by merely paying a mechanic so that he could come to fix it. When you have extra money saved, you can use it to make most problems go away and things like a car breaking down become just an annoyance instead of financial stress.

If you don't have any debt, then you don't have to worry if you will be able to cover your next installment and the life is just more fun when you don't have to worry about as many things and when you can focus on living presently and in the moment.

More Freedom

You are freer when you don't have to worry about all the things you have to maintain in order to make it through life. The interesting thing is that you don't need to concern yourself with your house being robbed while you're not at home since you don't have many things with you at one time in the first place.

Freedom is the key to being happy in life and it is not possible to be truly happy in life if you are limited and if there are a lot of things you are unable to do for arbitrary reasons.

The Power of Gratitude

There is more to happiness that can be gained from minimalism. Minimalism comes down to the realization that you have all that you need in order to be happy no matter what your current circumstances are. You don't need to constantly be chasing that next thing and then slowly going back to the default level of happiness once you acquire it. When you are constantly chasing the next thing, you will realize that you never really stop to smell the roses and to appreciate what you have.

What you have to train yourself to do is to develop an appreciation of how lucky you are already by living in such a prosperous time. You need to develop and practice gratitude. The simple way to achieve this is to take time and to think of everything you own and the reasons you should feel grateful because of that. It doesn't have to take more than a couple of minutes. It is good to have it written down in some kind of notepad so that you can remind yourself of that.

You want to try to add things to your gratitude list and you will get better at this over time since there are a lot of cool things to be grateful for. Your health is wealth and you should be grateful for that. You can be grateful if you have people who care about you. You can also be grateful for the fact that you have a place where you can spend your night.

In order to make being grateful easier, you want to regularly do things you enjoy by following the list of enjoyable activities which you compiled earlier. You have to be really enjoying the things on the list and it can be whatever you want, whether it's admiring the night sky or helping your kids build a sand castle.

You need some creativity when making this list so that you utilize the things you already have in order to have a good time. You only have to look around you a bit to get a lot of ideas on how to have a good time.

No matter what you do, you need to reflect on how happy you are to be in a situation that you are in. You want to get to the point when you are living presently and mindfully in the moment and not worrying about what's next or about what was and this is a pretty important spiritual concept. You don't want to allow your mind to go astray since that will inevitably lead you to your worries which will make it harder to enjoy what you are currently doing. When you are in a museum or an art gallery or someplace similar, you want to be able to truly appreciate what is in front of you.

Another challenge is to slow down during your breakfast so that you can actually take in and realize how much enjoyment you are actually getting out of it. You will also be enjoying your meal a whole lot more if you anticipate it beforehand. Regardless of what your meal will be, it will be so much better if you create some anticipation. It is all about knowing how to really appreciate good things in life and in this way you are letting more value into your life and this can be done regardless of how much money you have and this can be a difference between a non-wealthy person who is a happy and miserable wealthy person.

Conclusion

I hope that this book has provided you with an understanding of minimalism and the ways in which you can use it to make your life better. It may seem like all this book is about is removing some clutter here and there so that you can start to properly enjoy what is important to you. You have to know what you want out of life in order to formulate a plan that will get you there. Minimalism, however, is also about designing a home that serves you and which helps you in reaching your goals by making things easy for you via elimination of obstacles and clutter such as debt.

I hope that, by now, you have developed an inspiration for turning your home into something entirely new by just getting rid of the unnecessary stuff and the financial burden of having to keep it all together. I know that you have some unique ideas on how would you design your home so that it looks luxurious while also adding your own flavor to it.

But in order to do this, you first have to accept it in your mind that you don't need a lot in order to be happy regardless of what the media are telling you. The actual truth is that a lot of stuff which you have might actually be making you less happy and causing you stress and stopping you from doing what you truly want since your current expenses are so high.

A lot of things which you thought you wanted, you probably may not even have wanted since the idea of you wanting a certain item was placed in your head by advertising. You want to take control back and you can do so by creating a deliberate plan for achieving your vision. This way you will only be spending on what is getting you closer to the goal and the lifestyle which you want to have.

You need to be patient and to keep hope alive because one day you will break out of the loop of always wanting the next thing and your mindset will be transformed so that you could be happy. The whole process of going minimal is a journey and you can start it right now and without any cost by getting rid of those things you know don't serve you anymore.

I hope that you have enjoyed this book and that applying what you have just read will make you happier and more fulfilled. If you would like to share your thoughts on this book, then you can do so by leaving a review on the Amazon page. Have a great rest of the day!

Made in the USA
Lexington, KY
05 June 2019